Old PENICUIK

by
William F. Hendrie

Children and adults gather in front of the old stone and slate cottages in Esk Bridge for their photograph to be taken.

© William F. Hendrie 2002
First published in the United Kingdom, 2002,
by Stenlake Publishing
Telephone / Fax: 01290 551122

ISBN 1 84033 213 1

The publishers regret that they cannot supply copies of any pictures featured in this book.

ACKNOWLEDGEMENTS

I am most grateful to Jim and Jean Baird and Raeburn Young and her late husband, Willie, former president of Penicuik History Society, for all the assistance which they unstintingly gave me in gathering information for this book. My thanks also to Burns Scott, the Local Studies Librarian and staff of Midlothian Library Headquarters, the headmaster and staff of Wellington School, the Army Training Regiment, Glencorse Barracks, Edinburgh Crystal and my editor at Stenlake Publishing, Oliver van Helden.

The publishers would like to thank Aerofilms for permission to reproduce several aerial photographs in this book.

Spear Gate, Penicuik, was one of the lodge houses for Penicuik Estate.

INTRODUCTION

Penicuik is situated to the south of Edinburgh in the sheltering lee of the Pentland Hills. Its name means 'the place of the cuckoo' and this gives a clear indication of the rural nature of the surrounding area. The peaceful agricultural aspect of the district began, however, to change gradually from 1709 when one of Scotland's earliest women entrepreneurs, Mrs Agnes Campbell, widow of the royal printer and later Lady Roseburn, leased a site on the banks of the River Esk from the Penicuik Estate and became the first to harness its rushing waters to power a paper mill. Around 1770 the arrival of the famous Cowan family as mill owners resulted in a quickening of the pace of development, and the need for homes for their workers led to the hamlet of Penicuik expanding into a town, whose layout was controlled by local laird John Clerk through the leases of land which he granted.

Clerk was the grandson of John Clerk who acquired the lands around Penicuik when he purchased the estate of Newbiggin in 1646. John Clerk Jnr. was an MP who enjoyed the distinction of being created a baronet in 1679, but it was his son – also called John and born three years earlier in 1676 – who went on to achieve even greater fame as Scotland's leading arbiter of culture and taste at the start of the eighteenth century. A lawyer by profession, John Clerk benefited greatly from what he learned on an extended 'Grand Tour' of Europe which he made as a youth. He returned to Scotland with his imagination charged with all that he had seen, and his mind full of the challenging ideas of the age of the Enlightenment. Sir John became the country's leading patron of the arts and as befitted his position commissioned his protégé, Scottish architect William Adam, to design a modern version of a Greek Palladian villa where he could entertain his many visitors. The house, in whose planning and construction he took a very active interest, took over four years to build. Called Mavisbank, when completed on its site overlooking the North Esk in 1727 its elegant appearance and compact design defined a new style which was copied in the building of many future Scottish country mansions. However, Clerk never intended Mavisbank to be his main residence, and used to refer to it simply as his summer pavilion where he could converse with the likes of his friend, distinguished Scottish artist Allan Ramsay, to whom he was a patron.

In contrast to the elegance of Mavisbank, Penicuik's earliest buildings were much more modest, with single- and two-storeyed houses with forestairs lining the streets around the original parish kirk, whose tower still stands overlooking the later St Mungo's Church. A plan dated 1796 shows Bank Street with only three small buildings in it, and Back Mill Lands with only seven houses. There were thirteen buildings, large and small, in the Square, but the only part of Bridge Street that was in existence at the time was the portion between Thorburn Terrace and the exit from Back Mill Lands, and on that space only one house had been erected. What became the main road to Edinburgh via the Loan and John Street terminated at Cuiken Farm at the time, and the only route north to the city was by Kirkhill and Harpers Brae.

By 1800 the population of Penicuik had risen to 1,700 and the centre of the town had begun to take on the appearance which is still familiar today. With its unusual neoclassical facade, not to mention its stylish manse and stable block, St Mungo's forms a focal point at the end of Penicuik High Street. Many other interesting historic buildings are also situated here, including the Old Crown Inn, where Burke of body-snatching infamy is claimed to have drunk, and the Royal Hotel. As well as being the centre of Penicuik's social life, the latter also served as its first post office and coach departure point in the years when the town was growing in importance as an industrial centre with its prosperous paper and cotton mills and nearby coal pits. Sadly, in connection with the latter industry, Penicuik will always be remembered as the scene of the Mauricewood Disaster of 5 September 1889. Sixty-three miners died as a result of a blaze which swept through the underground workings at Mauricewood, the worst catastrophe in the history of mining in the Lothians.

Paper-making has long been an important local industry, and the following account of the process as carried out at Cowan's works in the nineteenth century provides a valuable insight into what it involved at that time. It was first published in the *Scotsman* in 1868.

> The buildings are so much detached and scattered that it is difficult to realise the extent of the Cowan family's operations. To proceed in proper order the rag store is the first to be visited. It is a substantial wooden two-storey building a hundred yards in length. Only the highest quality [rags] are used by Messrs. Cowan as all of the paper which they produce is of the finest kind. From the store the rags are transported to the cutting and sorting rooms where a large number of women are employed. Each woman stands in front of a bench, the upper surface of which is covered with wire netting. Taking a handful of rags from a bale she shakes them out on the bench and removes any pins and buttons before cutting them into

small pieces by drawing them over the blade of a huge knife fixed to the bench in a perpendicular position. The rags are next put through the cutting machine which consists of a cylinder covered with wire net with a series of pegs or spikes inside. To get rid of the remaining dirt and some of the colouring materials the rags are boiled in an alkaline solution in the boiling house which contains large cauldrons. The engines which then convert the rags into pulp were invented in Holland. During the operation which takes two hours a stream of pure water flows through the machine and carries off any impurities. When the washing and breaking in is completed the rags are deposited into bleaching vats where they are subjected to 24 hours of the action of chloride of lime leaving the fibres perfectly white. By pressure in a hydraulic press the bleaching liquor is extracted. Later the stuff is placed in the beating engine. After a further five hours the contents are drawn off into large shoots [sic] from which the paper making machines are supplied. Messrs. Cowan have five machines of which the latest is the largest and most modern in Britain. Including the drying apparatus it is 250 feet in length and is capable of turning out 2,500 square feet of paper in an hour. Before the web of semi-formed paper leaves the apron it passes through a wire roller on which letters or devices made of wire are sewn thus producing the water mark which helps prevent fraud.

With the exception of a paper mill which still operates at Milton Bridge, Penicuik's original industries have now largely disappeared. Nonetheless the town continues to prosper, largely because of its setting close to Edinburgh, which makes it an excellent base for commuters and has also proved a draw for new high-tech industries. One of the first new employers to establish itself in the town was Edinburgh Crystal, which chose to move from its original crowded one-acre city works at Norton Park in 1972. It now occupies a seven-and-a-half acre site to the north of Penicuik, and is the area's largest employer with a workforce of 250. Edinburgh Crystal has also brought the town considerable benefit through its spacious visitor centre, audio-visual display and factory tour, which have become popular tourist attractions.

With its attractive setting at the foot of the Pentland Hills on the banks of the River Esk, there were hopes in Victorian times that Penicuik might grow into an inland holiday resort, similar to its neighbour Peebles to the south. While these were never realised, Penicuik did gain a bustling vitality as a garrison town as a result of the siting of the military barracks on its outskirts at Glencorse. This military presence still ensures good business for the town's excellent selection of shops, hotels, restaurants and cafes, which make it a most pleasant place both to live in and visit. Community spirit is abundant in Penicuik, and this is illustrated to the full when on the last Saturday in May the Hunter and his Lass are installed. With the Hunter wearing a black silk top hat and decorated with a sash and rosette, and his Lass carrying his colours, the Hunter's song is sung to the tune of *Do Ye Ken John Peel*. The words of the song include the lines: 'The Bonnie Pentland Hills wi' their view sae grand, the March Burn, The River Esk are a' at oor command', aptly summing up the pride which the people of Penicuik take in their town and its surroundings. It is hoped that this selection of views of Penicuik taken during the early decades of the 1900s will interest residents and visitors alike, and give them a better idea of how the town has derived its present appearance and vitality.

BRIDGE STREET, PENICUIK.

Penicuik has one of the most open and spacious town centres in Scotland, seen to advantage in this view of the High Street taken during the first decade of the 1900s. A single horse-drawn cart and two cyclists make up the only traffic in what is today Penicuik's busiest thoroughfare. The neoclassical pillared facade of St Mungo's Parish Church forms a focal point in the centre background, while looming over the street to the right is the familiar clock and tower of the Cowan Institute.

Alexander Cowan, well-known local paper mill owner, gifted the Cowan Institute to the people of Penicuik – many of whom were his workers – but sadly died before it was officially opened by the Lord Provost of Edinburgh on 22 December 1894. It was built of pink Cumberland freestone in Scottish baronial style by local building contractors Tait & Co. to a design by architects Campbell, Douglas & Morrison. Now officially called Penicuik Town Hall, it is still affectionately referred to as the Institute by most of the town's older inhabitants. Its ornate stonework incorporates thistles and other Scottish symbols, while its crow-stepped gable, balcony, octagonal belfry and wrought iron bracketed clock combine to make it a most eye-catching and imposing municipal building.

The three-storey Royal Hotel, whose attractive facade is still the main feature of this side of Penicuik High Street, has offered refreshments to local inhabitants and travellers alike for over two centuries. It first opened on this site as the King's Arms and today its lounge and public bars and popular Font Stane Restaurant are under the direction of host Glen Faichney. Over the years the Royal has served as the town's first post office, fire station and coach terminus, as well as being the setting for dances and many other functions. Hotelier Mr J. Dodds, formerly licensee of the Old Railway Inn, once owned the Royal and was Penicuik's first postmaster. In 1817 he supervised the first dispatch of mail by horse-drawn coach to Edinburgh. While the Royal Hotel has survived practically unchanged down the years, the shop premises on the near side of what this postcard describes as Hotel Corner (the junction of John Street) have not, and this site is now occupied by the Clydesdale Bank. The Clydesdale traces its origins to the Edinburgh & Leith Bank, which was the first bank to open for business in Penicuik with Mr James Symington as 'bank agent', as the manager was originally described.

The Royal Hotel on the left, and the bracketed clock of the Cowan Institute on the right (added in 1901), both feature in this view of the Square and the High Street, although it is the well in the left foreground which dominates the scene. This was given to the town by the Cowan family in 1809 to ensure an adequate supply of pure drinking water, and the supply was further improved in 1864 by Mr Charles Cowan who was responsible for the erection of the present classical-style well-house with its public drinking fountain. To mark the occasion he donated a pair of pitchers (large china jugs) to be given to the first bride who as a married woman carried water home from the well. The pitchers were won by Isabel Burton following her marriage to local baker John Donaldson. The Cowans were also responsible for the introduction of a gas supply to Penicuik. Gas was manufactured from coal at a plant at the family's Valleyfield Paper Mills from 1830, and five years later was used to light Penicuik Parish Church. The Penicuik District Gas Co. was founded in 1877 and provided a supply of gas to private homes and businesses as well as to the lamps which lit the streets of the town.

The Co-op's central premises on the corner of the High Street in the Square are seen here after they were rebuilt following the fire of 1904. The new Co-op buildings incorporated this more modern facade with balustrade and decorative clock. Today the building is occupied by privately-owned shops. The Railway Tavern is situated in the adjoining premises, while the two-storey building with the distinctive row of first floor windows now houses the More Store. The shop with the white awning protecting the goods in its window has long-since been demolished and replaced by a branch of the Clydesdale Bank. This is situated on the corner of John Street, the entrance to which was widened when the bank was built.

Penicuik's tree-lined High Street was still devoid of traffic when this photograph was taken from St Mungo's Parish Church looking south into the Square. Businesses which flourished in this part of the town included Johnston the baker, Kelling's fish and chip shop and Aikman the printer. They were all drawn together in a curious manner through the enterprise of Penicuik native John Strang who, following a visit to the USA, returned and persuaded his fellow businessmen to establish a football pools gambling enterprise long before the famous Littlewoods, Murphy's or Vernons were in business. Aikman printed the coupons, Kelling's sold them and Johnston's bakery in John Street was used on Saturday evenings after the matches to count the points and decide the dividends. As interest in his innovative football pools widened, Strang moved the business to premises in Leith where it was eventually taken over by larger rival Murphy's – although for a time it was Penicuik which led the country in this gambling enterprise. Despite being initially illegal, it generated as much interest as the modern Lotto in its day.

Looking in the opposite direction towards St Mungo's Parish Church, this later view still shows only one car in Penicuik High Street, in sharp contrast to its now almost constant flow of traffic. St Mungo's came into use in 1771 and its Georgian style manse with stone-built stables and coach house stands adjacent to it. The manse still bears its original title of the Glebe, the name of the land granted to ministers to enable them to either grow crops or generate extra income by leasing the land to a farmer, thereby augmenting their stipend. A subscription fund to pay for the round clock in the centre of the pediment of the church was begun by the Cowan family and contributed to by many of Penicuik's residents.

The tower of Penicuik's earlier parish kirk still stands overlooking the graveyard behind St Mungo's Church. As a result of its proximity to Edinburgh and the city's famous university medical school, there was considerable fear in Penicuik during the first half of the nineteenth century that its kirkyard might well be visited by the dreaded resurrectionists, who stole corpses and sold them to anatomists for dissection. Most famous of the much-feared body-snatchers were Burke and Hare, and Burke is reputed to have lived in a house on the south side of Penicuik High Street, regularly visiting the Old Crown Inn next door. The local inhabitants took no chances, and to prevent any risk of their loved-one's remains being removed after a burial relatives sat on guard at the kirkyard for three weeks, after which the body would had deteriorated to such an extent that it would be of no use for dissection. Twenty-one nights was an exhaustingly long period for relatives to maintain their graveside vigil, so they sometimes employed elderly local men to sit up in their place. It was said that the payment was always a bottle of whisky, allegedly to keep up their spirits! In 1678 the minister and elders of Penicuik Parish Church had to deal with a case of alleged witchcraft when Margaret Dickson accused John Henderson of Howgate 'of working his ale with a dead man's skull'. Later after questioning she confessed that this was untrue, and to indicate the seriousness of the offence was ordered to appear upon her knees before the members of the session.

Fear of crime was as great in the nineteenth century as it is in modern times, and a reflection of this was the building of Wellington School near Penicuik. With its grim facade, fronted by high iron railings, this was a school no Penicuik boy ever wanted to attend. Dating from 1859, it was established as a reform school to cater for delinquent youths, mainly from Edinburgh's city streets. Despite its fearsome reputation, Wellington was considered at the time to offer an enlightened approach to the treatment of young offenders. Previously thieves and other juvenile delinquents had simply been flogged – and frequently incarcerated alongside adult criminals. Victorian social reformers considered it would be more humane to send young offenders to residential industrial schools where they could be taught a useful trade. The hope was that their charges could be 'duly reformed', as the 1856 Act of Parliament which established the schools phrased it. In Scotland the campaign to establish reform schools was led by Sheriff Cleghorn. On seeking suitable premises for a school, he discovered an old coaching inn for sale on the road from Penicuik to Peebles. The price was cheap as the coming of the railway had reduced the number of coach passengers. Cleghorn purchased the inn and leased its site to a board of trustees – with the assurance that it was far enough from Penicuik to not upset the neighbours. The first boy on the roll of Wellington School was James Watt, who was admitted in February 1860 after being found guilty of stealing a small bottle of hair oil from a barber's shop in Edinburgh's High Street.

The interior of one of the workshops at Wellington School with the boys at their workbenches. When it first opened under the headmastership of John Craste (whose wife acted as matron), the original 40 inmates were taught joinery. In 1862 the boy carpenters constructed a wooden bridge across the River Esk at Valleymills, whose owner, Mr Cowan, was one of Wellington's governors. Two years later the boys built a wooden pulpit and a baptismal font for Penicuik South Church, which they were forced to attend every Sunday, being marched two miles there and two miles back again in a long column to participate in worship. By 1865 the number of boys resident at Wellington had soared to 100 and it became necessary to find alternative work to keep them gainfully occupied. In 1870 Mosshouses Farm was acquired and within two years the inmates had 230 acres under cultivation with 50 cows, seven horses and two ponies. A shop was opened in Cockburn Street off Edinburgh's Royal Mile to sell the food which they produced. Within Wellington itself however the diet was frugal. The boys rose at 6 a.m. and 30 minutes later breakfast of porridge was served before they started work at 7 a.m. Lunch consisted of pease meal. Work ended at 6 p.m. after which bowls of vegetable soup were served as an evening meal. The only variation from this basic menu was the addition of fatty mutton twice weekly.

In addition to farming and joinery the other main trade taught at Wellington was shoemaking. Amongst their output the boys produced stout leather tackety boots which they wore themselves. On occasion the leather with which they worked was also used by the master in charge to make a thick punishment strap, because while Wellington was originally established to decrease the number of birchings ordered by the courts, corporal punishment was a regular feature of the school's strict regime. Unlike in ordinary schools in Scotland, beatings were administered across the boys' bottoms in judicial fashion and the punishment book bears silent witness to thrashings varying from three strokes for misbehaviour in the dormitories to six strokes for daring to run away, all inflicted as Scottish Office regulations decreed 'through ordinary cloth trousers'. Corporal punishment was, however, finally suspended at Wellington by a controversially liberal new headmaster in 1969, almost two decades before the belt was finally abolished in all Scottish local authority schools in 1987.

With its eye-catching architecture, Penicuik South UF Church in Peebles Road was a strikingly modern new building when the boys of Wellington Reform School were paraded there for worship in the 1860s. Its construction came about as a result of the Disruption, the famous unholy row which split the Church of Scotland at its General Assembly in St Andrew's Church in George Street, Edinburgh, in 1843. Around half of the ministers and their elders walked out of the meeting to protest against lairds being allowed to decide who should fill pulpits instead of the choice being that of members of their congregations. The result was the establishment of the Free Church, whose members in Penicuik first built premises in West Street. These are still used as the South Church hall, and the minister's home, the manse, is adjacent to them.

This very impressive successor to the original Free Kirk premises in West Street was constructed in 1862 as a result of the grant of the site by Sir George Clerk. Designed by eminent architect Thomas Frederick Pilkington, also responsible for the well-known Barclay Church in Bruntsfield, Edinburgh, it cost £2,050 to erect and had pews to seat 700 worshippers. These were filled to capacity on 24 March 1880 when the famous Liberal politician and future British Prime Minister, William Ewart Gladstone, spoke there during his famous Midlothian campaign. The crowded meeting was chaired by mill-owner Charles Cowan, and Gladstone was duly elected as Member of Parliament for the area. The most famous minister at Penicuik South Church was the Scottish author Samuel Rutherford Crockett. Born in 1859 in Balmaghie, Kirkcudbrightshire, he studied at Edinburgh's divinity school, New College, and became minister at Penicuik in 1886. Married to the daughter of a Manchester mill-owner and nonconformist philanthropist, he and his wife raised their family of four children in Penicuik, where Crockett courted controversy by championing the cause of better conditions for paper mill workers and coal miners. After the Mauricewood Pit disaster in 1889 he organised extensive relief for the families of the 63 miners who were killed. Four years later Crockett's publication *The Stickit Minister*, exposing the hypocrisy of many of his fellow preachers, brought him sudden fame. He went on to write several hugely popular novels including *Men of the Moss Hags* (about the Covenantors) and *Cleg Kelly*, in which he exposed the squalor of the Edinburgh slums. After becoming a United Free Church, Penicuik South Church and many of its fellow UF churches rejoined the Church of Scotland in 1929.

Although now bereft of its spire, Penicuik's original Free Church building – on the left of this view – still stands in West Street. The postcard dates from the early years of the twentieth century when horse-drawn carts and carriages were still the only vehicles in the town, and Penicuik's streets were illuminated by flickering gas lamps of the sort seen on either side of the street. Also featured are the two prosperous shops owned by Mr W. Simpson, one of whose descendants later became provost of the town. Mr Simpson owned a combined booksellers and stationers, from which this postcard may originally have been sold, as well as the adjoining drapers and hosiers. The shop with the pillared facade further along the street, beyond the covered pend between the buildings, is now the Wine Shop.

The district council offices dominate the left-hand corner of West Street and its junction with the Square. From these neat Scottish baronial style offices, the councillors and their clerk and officials were responsible for rural affairs in the country areas around Penicuik, although not in the town itself. The building did, however, house the town's registrar of births, marriages and deaths – or matches, hatches and dispatches as local people often referred to them. Following Scottish local government reorganisation in 1975 the offices have acquired an unexpected international role. As a result of Belgian national, Yves Lemarchand, marrying a woman from Penicuik, they now house the Belgian consulate in Scotland. A hotelier by profession, Mr Lemarchand has established a successful tourist business in the town. The offices which he occupies have changed little in appearance over the years although the tall flagstaff on the roof has been replaced by another from which the red, yellow and black flag of Belgium now flies, while after the lamp above the entrance was knocked off by a lorry the ornate wall bracket was put to good use bearing the Belgian heraldic coat of arms. The offices were also previously the town's civil defence HQ and when Mr Lemarchand took over the premises he found a supply of camp beds, water containers and cookery utensils locked in a cupboard for use in an emergency. Another interesting occupant of modern West Street is Penicuik Community Arts, which celebrated its 25th anniversary in 2002. It holds evening demonstrations, discussions and lectures in its popular cafe and shop and hosts regular exhibitions in its gallery of work by local people, from craftsmen to the drawings of local personalities by Penicuik-based cartoonist Doreen Cullen.

BRIDGE STREET, PENICUIK

Children stopped to stare as the photographer set up his camera and took this attractive view looking north up the length of Bridge Street. The distinctive building on the right was known as The Nunnery as it was built by the Cowan family and part of it was used to house many of their young female employees. Designed by architect Thomas Frederick Pilkington, who was also responsible for the town's South Church, its official name was Park End. Apart from the removal of its little steeple, the external appearance of Park End has changed little in over a century. The premises whose window displays behind the five arches were protected by the white awnings in this view are now occupied by a well-stocked needlework, wool and crafts shop, which attracts customers to the town from the surrounding area. On the opposite side of the street the entrance to Cairnbank Road can be glimpsed.

As a result of the strict rules imposed by the paternalistic Cowan family, the part of Park End which the girl workers occupied was also sometimes referred to as The Cloister, although far from being cut off from the rest of the town it was actually in one of Penicuik's busiest shopping streets. In its heyday Bridge Street was home to Bell's Dairy, the post office, a newsagents, tobacconists, butchers and grocery. Nowadays one of the street's most interesting tenants is the Pen-y-Coe Press which publishes the very informative monthly free sheet, *The Town Crier*. Other well-known businesses and traders in past decades in Penicuik included Leiper the baker whose family came from Austria, and J. P. Thomson the dispensing chemist who served the patients of well-known local GP Dr Baldwin.

A car climbs the steep incline of Peebles Road to the south of Penicuik. The coming of motor vehicles increased the danger of road accidents, and one of the worst to happen in Penicuik occurred during the 1920s when a lorry descending this hill suffered brake failure and crashed through the stone parapet of the Telford Bridge, hurtling to its destruction in the River Esk below. The driver and a passenger were killed, although the young apprentice riding in the back managed to escape by clinging to the branch of an overhanging tree.

These two cottages still stand beside the Telford Bridge on the opposite side to that which the lorry crashed through. The angle of the approach of the road to the bridge (named after the famous Scottish engineer who designed it) was altered following the crash.

The Railway Inn serves as a reminder that Penicuik used to have rail connections to Edinburgh and Peebles. Rail travel first reached the area in 1855 when a station was built on the outskirts of the town at Pomathorn by the Peebles Railway Company. In 1861 the line between Edinburgh and Peebles was taken over by the much larger North British Railway, but it was not until 1871 that Penicuik station was opened. Two heavily laden horse-drawn carts are pictured outside the Railway Inn here, while a hand cart makes up the only traffic in the street in front of it. The inn was operated by the well-known Wilson family who also owned a grain store in the town. When the photograph was taken Henderson's family grocers occupied the premises now used by the Castle Warehouse, while on the opposite corner below the gas lamp there is another grocer's shop. Beyond it on the right a barber's pole juts out.

The steep descent into Penicuik from the south is captured in this photograph of the town taken from Pomathorn with the Pentland Hills in the background. In the foreground on the banks of the River Esk are the mills which brought work and prosperity to Penicuik. The old schoolhouse, built by the Cowans and opened in 1840 to help educate their young employees, can be seen just to the left of centre. Around 80 girls and 40 boys were compelled to attend evening classes after work for three months each winter. The Cowans were considered very enlightened employees and had provided lessons for their employees since 1823, insisting that all must learn to read, write and count while girls also had to master sewing.

Penicuik's famous paper mills are seen to advantage in this spectacular aerial view. Cowan's Valleyfield Mills were established in 1779, but a mill existed on this site from 1709 when paper-making was started in the town by Mrs Agnes Campbell, whose husband had been a printer by royal appointment to Queen Anne. In 1757 Charles Cowan, originally a grocer in Leith, married Marjorie Fidler, whose family had been exiled because of their support of the Jacobites in the 1745 uprising. As he prospered he used his wealth to purchase the mill in Penicuik and in 1796 brought his son Alex into the family business to manage it. Charles Cowan bought an adjacent corn mill in 1803 which became known as the Bank Mill after he converted it specially to produce the paper on which banknotes were printed. He expanded the business still further in 1815 by buying the nearby Low Mill from an Edinburgh man called Nimmo.

During the Napoleonic Wars, Britain's prolonged conflict with France at the start of the nineteenth century, the government found itself with an ever-growing number of French prisoners to accommodate. In 1803 it purchased the ground on which Glencorse Barracks now stands from Greenlaw estate for £10,000 as a convenient site on which to house POWs, it being within marching distance of the port of Leith. A convalescent camp for wounded British seamen was also established. The war against France proved to be much more prolonged than expected, however, and by the start of 1811 the original few hundred prisoners had grown to number almost 6,000. In February of that year the government purchased the huge premises of the Esk Mills, illustrated here, as alternative accommodation. After only six weeks a mass escape attempt led to the deaths of two prisoners and the authorities decided instead to rehouse the remaining men at the Valleyfield Mills, seen in the previous picture. In March work commenced on their conversion into what was at the time the largest POW camp in Scotland. The number of prisoners continued to rise, and with more accommodation desperately needed six large new wooden prison blocks were hastily erected in the grounds of Valleyfield. Alex Cowan's mansion was even acquired to provide hospital facilities. The entire POW camp was surrounded with a stout wooden stockade which was patrolled by members of the Ayrshire and Kirkcudbright Militias. There was much sympathy for the plight of the Frenchmen in Scotland and after the war, having repurchased the mills from the government for £2,200, Alex Cowan erected an impressive monument which still stands to their memory in the former mill grounds. Commemorative services are held there regularly, the most recent one being in July 2002.

This aerial photograph gives an idea of the extent of James Brown & Co.'s Esk Mills, which remained in production until 1968. Situated on the North Esk, the mills' machinery was originally powered by the river's fast flowing waters. Cowan's mills continued in operation until 1975, employing 600 people and producing up to 3,000 tons of paper per year. One of the company's chimneys – 240 feet in height and built in 1924 by local contractors – was demolished in 1976 with Penicuik steeplejack, Joe Pendreich, in charge of the operation. The light coloured field in the background of this picture is the site of the modern Ladywood Housing Estate.

At the top of this aerial view the tower of the original Parish Church is visible looming over the buildings of St Mungo's Church, with the minister's manse to the right, beyond which stretch the paper mills. In the centre are the premises of the Royal Hotel with its coach houses and stables. To their left is Hay's Garage. The open space behind is Hay's Park where many local football teams played their matches. The first mention of football occurs in 1882 when Parish Priest Father Boston founded a team named The Emmett. Britannic Star FC was started the following year and after playing for a season at Kirkhill Park moved to Hay's Park, which was then known as Royal Hotel Park. At a meeting in the hotel in 1888 the Star agreed to become Penicuik Athletic, a name which has lived on in the town ever since. In 1930 Penicuik Athletic FC joined the East of Scotland League and in 1948 the team re-formed and moved to its new ground at Eastfield. Up until the 1950s local football fans unable to attend a game frequently telephoned the town's manual exchange to ask the operators for the half time and full time scores.

Penicuik's famous mills lie in the centre background of this view, with John Street prominent on the left and Jackson Street parallel and to the right. The foot of the latter is where the town's war memorial now stands, at the entrance to the public park, although it was originally sited in the High Street. Jackson Street is one of Penicuik's most pleasant residential areas, lined with fine stone-built detached, semi-detached and terraced houses. Many properties in the street were built by the well-known local building firm of Tait & Co., who also built the Cowan Institute. A distinctive tenement with latticed windows, designed by R. S. Naismith, stands in John Street. The open space at the top left-hand side of the photograph is Hay's Park.

The curve of John Street is still recognisable from this photograph, taken in the years before the Second World War, although at its High Street end it has since been pedestrianised. The two men wearing overalls may have been working for Wilson's, a well-known local firm of house painters and interior decorators. The Presbytery of the Roman Catholic Church still stands in John Street, which was also formerly home to the headquarters of the Salvation Army. Shortly after its establishment in Penicuik, the Salvation Army won much public praise for the immediate practical help given by its members to the victims of the 1889 Mauricewood colliery disaster. Bank Street leads off to the left.

Many of the attractive houses seen in this tree-framed view of Kirkhill Road, a number of which were built to accommodate workers from Esk Mills, still stand today. St Mungo's Church Hall has since been built on the site occupied by the trees on the left; the Volunteer Hall was previously situated near here. Penicuik's YMCA and YWCA, which provide many activities for young people in the town and the surrounding areas, are at the top of Kirkhill Road. The small white building in the middle distance was a garage, and the town's burgh boundary line was located midway up Kirkhill.

John Street and Jackson Street feature again in this aerial photograph. On the original postcard someone has written the word 'McGregor's' and added an arrow pointing to the school (centre foreground); Mr McGregor was such a formidable headmaster that the school which he ran in Jackson Street was usually referred to by his name. In 1869 Mr McGregor was the successor to Penicuik's first dominie, Robert Alexander, of whom the following was written: 'He was a kind-hearted man, an excellent scholar and a successful teacher when he had bright pupils. The duller spirits however did not progress so rapidly under his tuition, although he was never backward in stimulating their efforts by a free application of the tawse. Sadly Mr Alexander, while in the midst of a lesson, collapsed and died in front of his pupils.' Sacred Heart School, Penicuik's Roman Catholic Church and Ferrier's Foundry were all situated on Jackson Street.

"The Clipping Time," Fallhills, Penicuik.

One of the country chores which may well have caught the attention of the city lads who came to camp at Coats Farm (inside front cover) was the annual shearing of the sheep. Here the clipping is seen in progress at another local farm, Fallhills, to which livestock have been driven from their grazing grounds on the Pentland Hills. Those in the background still have their fleeces while the ones in the foreground are in the process of being shorn. Note in the middle of the picture the woman wearing the long white apron who may well have been the farmer's wife, and on the right the ever-watchful collie dog ready to round up any sheep which might dare to stray. Clipping was strenuous work and the day long, but at the end of it there was always a good home-cooked meal waiting ready for the shearers when they returned to the farmhouse. Note the tidy haystacks in the background.

Penicuik's public park was officially opened by Provost Wilson in 1904; this picture shows the entrance at the west end of Jackson Street, and was taken after the town's war memorial had been removed from the High Street and re-erected here in 1927. The child in the centre is riding a Wee Willie Winkie tricycle which may have been supplied by Penicuik's well-known Baird's Garage, which belonged to the Raleigh Five Hundred Club because it established such a large trade in the sale of bicycles. The garage was originally opened by John Dodds in 1911. Mrs Baird, the garage owner's wife, also took over the little corner shop originally run by the Wood family. The shop seen on the far side of the playing field served as the unofficial tuck shop for pupils of Penicuik High School and was famed for its home-made sticky toffee apples. Mr Purslow, the park's first gardener, was nicknamed The Waup by local children because they claimed he had eyes like a curlew and could spot any mischief that they thought about before they dared get up to it!

Now called Penicuik High School, this fine building was known as Penicuik Public School when it opened in 1938. It replaced McGregor's School in Jackson Street and several small outlying schools whose primary pupils were transferred to the new premises. With its large windows and south facing classrooms ranged on either side of the main entrance facing Penicuik public park, it was considered to be the most up-to-date of educational architectural designs. The park provided space for PT – physical training or physical torture as the pupils often nicknamed it – and pitches for team sports as indicated by the rugby posts seen on the left. The school, however, also had an indoor gymnasium with rows of wall bars, which has considered very up-to-date provision in those pre-Second World War days. Within two years the outbreak of war impinged on the new school when Edinburgh children were evacuated to the town. Air raid shelters were hurriedly erected in case of an attack during school hours. In addition to Penicuik High School, the town is now also served by Beeslack High School, which is situated on its northern outskirts.

Penicuik has strong connections with the army through its presence at Glencorse Barracks. Built in the grounds of Greenlaw House, the barracks, seen here, originated as a POW camp to house French servicemen during the Napoleonic Wars. When hostilities ended in 1815 it became a transit camp for the British Army. In 1845 the camp reverted to being a prison but this time for army offenders. Finally in 1873 it became a training depot, a role which it continued to fulfil until its closure for refurbishment in 2002. Buildings added in 1873 included the Keep which was built originally as an armoury and housed 3,000 small arms and equipment. In 1902 Glencorse was officially named as the Depot of the Royal Scots, the regiment with which it has been most closely connected over the last century. New buildings and facilities were added at this time including a gymnasium. After the Second World War the Royal Military Police and Royal Corps of Signals used Glencorse successively from 1948 to 1954, then for the next six years it once again became the Depot of the Royal Scots. In 1960 it was largely rebuilt as Lowland Brigade Depot. The regiments of the Lowland and Highland Brigades combined in 1969 when Glencorse became the depot for adult recruits to Scottish Division. The barracks are scheduled to reopen in 2005 following the present extensive upgrade programme.

House o' Muir Cottages still stand at Glencorse. This was the birthplace of Mrs Margaret Graham, whose son continues the family tradition of farming at Ravensneuk on the outskirts of Penicuik.

A lone soldier pedals past Logan Bank lodge house at Milton Bridge near the barracks at Glencorse on the northern outskirts of Penicuik.

This postcard was sent by a Miss Aitken from Dalmore Cottage, which stood at the entrance to the paper mill at Auchendinny on the outskirts of Penicuik. It shows Milton Bridge with a horse-drawn cart forming the only traffic on the street. Milton Bridge always had a very busy sub-post office because of the amount of official mail sent by the regiment in residence at Glencorse, and also all of the love letters and postcards sent by the officers and men at the barracks.

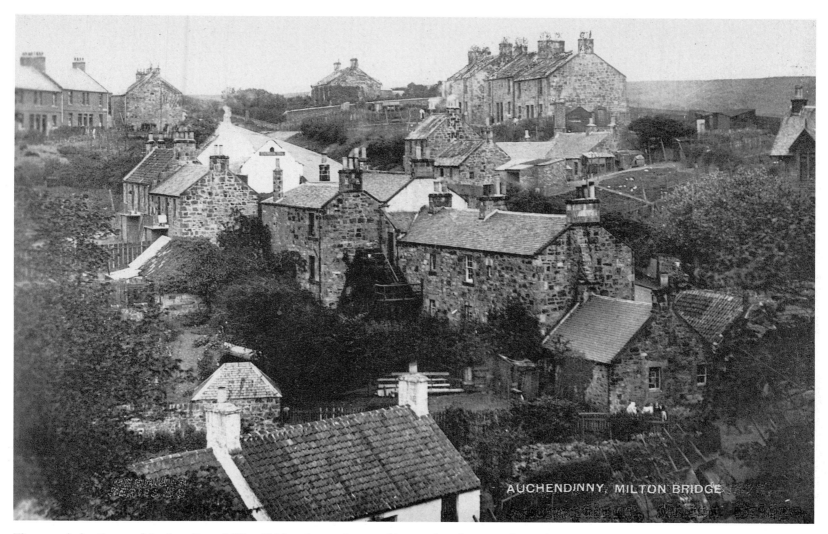

The crowded cottages of Auchendinny, Milton Bridge, form a jigsaw of interesting shapes in this early photograph of its steeply sloping riverbank site. Auchendinny is nicknamed the paper-making village. Curtis Fine Papers still operate at Milton Bridge where their Dalmore Mill employs approximately 130 staff. Last year's output was about 8,000 tons of fine paper.

Called The Bush, this fine mansion on the outskirts of Penicuik originally belonged to the Trotter family, whose crest can still be seen on some of the wrought iron railings. The front entrance is situated below the curved balustrade of the two-storey facade on the right, although much of the house has a third floor whose rooms with their dormer windows formerly accommodated the many servants needed to ensure the smooth running of such a large and impressive country home. The Bush still stands at Milton Bridge where it is the headquarters of the agricultural department of the University of Edinburgh. Its grounds are home to Scotland's first 'biocampus' where a number of high-tech firms have already established a presence. The Pentlands business park and conference centre and the University of Edinburgh's famous Dick Veterinary Hospital are also situated nearby.

THE VIADUCT, MILTON BRIDGE.

Architect Thomas Bouch of Tay Bridge infamy designed the viaduct which formerly carried the railway line across the river at Milton Bridge. Fortunately, however, his viaduct near Penicuik stood the test of time, unlike the ill-fated Tay Bridge. It was opened in 1877 and stood for 110 years. During the time that it spanned the valley players at Glencorse golf course enjoyed the considerable challenge of hitting a ball over the top of it. The viaduct was demolished in 1987, 28 years after the last train passed over it in 1959. Passenger services had been withdrawn before this date and Glencorse station's single-storey premises were demolished during the 1950s.

Penicuik House, dating from 1761, was designed on a grand scale by James Clerk. He was the eldest son and heir of one of Penicuik's most famous residents, Sir John Clerk, the early eighteenth century lawyer and distinguished Scottish man of letters who designed Mavisbank in collaboration with the architect William Adam. This is an unusual view of the rear of this once impressive mansion. Following the gutting by fire of Penicuik House in 1899, the Clerk family moved into the mansion's stable block.

Now the Navaar Hotel, this distinctive building was originally called the Bungalow and later went by the name of Redgables. It was once the home of Professor James Cossar Ewart, who while occupying the chair of natural history at the University of Edinburgh conducted his famous Penicuik experiments in the stables of this building. These consisted of cross-breeding horses with zebras and then later with horses again to discover whether the stripes of the father were exhibited by the subsequent offspring. His theory of telegony, which was proved false, was intended to enable the breeding of stock which would be resistant to pests such as tsetse in the countries of the expanding British Empire in Africa and Asia. In 1885 Professor Ewart moved to neighbouring Craigiebield, which was designed by his brother, a well-known architect. Like the Navaar, Craigiebield is now a popular Penicuik hotel on whose lawns marquees are often erected to cater for large wedding receptions and other functions.

This 1920s picture shows the village of Howgate on the southern outskirts of Penicuik, with the well-known Howgate Inn at its heart. Following the Second World War the Garard family established the inn as a popular eating place which attracted guests from Edinburgh as well as the local area. After a fire it did not reopen for business and has now been converted into private houses.

In 1743 the Laird of Penicuik leased the Howgate Inn for 999 years. A coach plied daily from the inn to Candlemakers' Row in Edinburgh, while its situation ten miles from the centre of Edinburgh meant that it was also the first place where coaches on the longer routes to Peebles and the south changed their horses. The large lantern above the entrance would have acted as a beacon to travellers, who on arrival may have been greeted by the two gentlemen photographed here, accompanied in this picture by the inn's cat and dog. Beyond the curved coach-house door on the left is a water butt.

Scottish author Dr John Brown brought fame to the Carrier's Quarters at Howgate when he based his famous story *Rab and His Friends* on the family who lived there and their faithful dog. The carriers operated a regular goods service between here and Candlemakers' Row in Edinburgh.

A lone car drives through the hamlet of Silverburn, which is situated at the foot of the Pentland Hills on the outskirts of Penicuik. Silverburn takes its name from the pure, clear water of the local stream which was supplied to the well in the High Street, donated by the Cowan family. The hamlet is situated on the main road between Edinburgh and Carlisle, and for many years there was a blacksmith's forge here which was kept busy providing new shoes for horses on this well-used route.

The Pentland Hills dominate this view of Silverburn taken during the 1920s. Two centuries earlier the Pentlands were the scene of much Covenantor activity when many Scots signed the National Covenant indicating their refusal to

have Episcopalian ways of worship forced upon them. So strong was their determination that they walked out of their churches and worshipped instead in the open air in the hills at what became known as conventicles. The government deemed this illegal, so lookouts were posted to warn of the approach of the redcoat soldiers. To try to prevent the Covenantors from gaining an early warning by spotting the distinctive redcoats from a distance, General Tam Dalyell sent to the Netherlands for bales of grey cloth with which to make uniforms for the regiment which he founded at his home, the House of the Binns near Linlithgow, in 1681. Thus it became known as the Royal Scots Greys. It was the first regiment in the British Army to be formed as a royal regiment from its beginnings, and the first to wear camouflage.

The Leadburn Inn is still a popular hotel on the outskirts of Penicuik at the junction of the roads to Dalkeith and Peebles. The inn is mentioned in the first novel written by John Buchan of *The Thirty-Nine Steps* fame. In his book *John Burnet of Barns*, Buchan writes, 'I came to Leadburn about eleven o'clock in the forenoon, somewhat cold in body but brisk and comforted in spirit. I had Maisie stabled and myself went into the hostel and bade them get ready dinner. The inn is the most villainous bleak place I have ever seen and I who write this have seen many. The rooms are damp mouldy and the chimney stacks threaten hourly to come down about the heads of the inmates. It stands in the middle of a black peat bog which stretches nie to the Pentland Hills and if there be a more forsaken countryside on earth, I do not know it. The landlord nevertheless was an active civil man, not spoiled by his surroundings and he fetched me an excellent dinner.' The landlord's present-day successor, Adrian Dempsey, is sufficiently confident of the equal excellence of his modern fare to quote the whole of Buchan's reference to his premises on his menus, and the modern appearance of the inn and surrounding area certainly belies the author's bleak description of it.

Leadburn station was on the Galashiels to Rosewell line and closed on 7 November 1955. This picture shows Leadburn station house.

A scene of rural tranquility at Leadburn Farm, with the farmer and his wife standing either side of the farm gate, their sheepdog looking on and hens pecking for food in farmyard behind them.